CW00996380

Elizabeth Barrett

WALKING
ON TIPTOE

Staple
NEW WRITING
1998

WALKING ON TIPTOE

Elizabeth Barrett

NO PART OF THIS PUBLICATION
MAY BE REPRODUCED, STORED
ON A RETRIEVAL SYSTEM, OR
TRANSMITTED, IN ANY FORM
OR BY ANY MEANS, WITHOUT
PRIOR PERMISSION IN WRITING
OF THE PUBLISHERS.

©
Elizabeth Barrett
1998

ISBN 1 901185 00 1

TYPESET
by
ROGER BOOTH ASSOCIATES
HASSOCKS, WEST SUSSEX
IN NEW BASKERVILLE

PRINTED
at
THE ARC & THROSTLE PRESS
NANHOLME MILL, TODMORDEN

DESIGN
by
BILL AND LUCY BERRETT

EDITORIAL BOARD
DAVID DUNCOMBE
DONALD MEASHAM
JOHN SEWELL
BOB WINDSOR

PUBLISHED
by
Staple NEW WRITING
15 JULY 1998

Staple
is published with
financial assistance
from East Midlands
Arts

For Dylan Ariel

CONTENTS

I CROOKED TIMBER

II WALKING ON TIPTOE

I CROOKED TIMBER

Out of timber so crooked as that from which man is made nothing entirely straight can be carved.

Immanuel Kant, Idee zu einer allgemeinen Geschichte in weltbürgerlicher Absicht (1784)

MRS EGON SCHIELE'S COMPLAINT

It is not a beautiful dress;
the muslin falls stiffly and the sash is too narrow.
But it has lines of the palest gentian,
fine stripes of cornflower.
And, if I stand very still,
perhaps he will see these cool blues
and give me their distance and mystery.
Perhaps, this time, he will not use familiar tones.

It is my strangeness he steals,
funnelling away the ice, making me hot with his reds.
He has flamed me with scarlet, magenta, damask and cochineal,
with the cardinal and carmine.
He has veiled me in Venetian Red and robed me in ruby;
my dresses have metamorphosed to crimson and maroon.
And, always, he puts the same colour in my hair:
'the loveliness of chestnut locks, my Titian sweet!'

If I close my eyes I can imagine away the auburn tresses
but, just once, I want him to see my blueness.
Today, I have mixed his palette. I have given him cobalt and marine.
There is azure, sapphire and lapis lazuli.
I have made him indigo for the bodice and navy for the sash.
For the cap, a Prussian Blue.
I compose myself: smooth my dress, tidy my hair.
Now, his footstep on the stair...

YELLOW CAR

This opens with her crying,
driving their old yellow car south,
white knuckles squeezing sobs from the hard wheel.

After four years, she can't go a step further.
But he doesn't know, yet, that she is leaving for good
(ever else always someone)

and that tonight, after the late movie,
trying hard not to think of her,
he will open their wardrobe door

to hang his shirt, cry –
cry that moment –
when he sees she has taken all her clothes.

They are piled in the back of that yellow car;
offering her new words, different ways of talking.
Tomorrow, she will try them out,

trying not to remember his brave goodbye
threading its clear vowels across the miles,
hoping these would drive her back.

All this was a long time ago now,
years since the engine went on her old yellow car,
but it ends with her still crying.

SHREDS

When they told him (together)
they had been sleeping with each other
he thought it wouldn't matter as much
as the way he loved her.
But, on the ninth day,
he took scissors from the kitchen drawer,
cut himself, carefully –
shoulders, jaw, cheeks, hair –
from all their photographs,
then replaced the glass.
His black sockets watched while she smiled
and he searched the bookshelves,
trying to remember her birthdays.
On the fly leaf of *Rip Van Winkle* (February 89)
he scrawled *only a bad dream.*
On the others, he scribbled black zig zags
through his name.
There was only one more to find
when he remembered the basque.

He hadn't known how to ask for it;
had chosen, awkwardly,
heady in a clutter of silks and straps,
the cerise lace.
They had been shy and excited before the fire
as she unwrapped it (December 85).
This vision of her was his. Could belong only to him.
He opened the thin drawer of her white chest,
slipped his hands, gently, beneath the waist,
laid the basque on their bed,
lowered himself, slowly, to kneel.
He fastened every hook,
turned it around,
buried his face where her breasts had been,
ran hands across her ribs.
He straightened the four straps for her thighs,
smoothed out the lace.

                    *

When she looked for it, months later,
trying to fix the shreds of her life,
it was the hooks that puzzled her most.
She undid them slowly, trying to remember.

THE ONION

He was visiting his best friend for a long weekend,
trying to keep things as normal as possible
having fallen into sex with his best friend's girl
(for at this stage it was really nothing more than that –
though he wanted the more, had been seduced
by all his friend had had these years;
the simplicity of sleeping together, waking to each other,
not the complicated stealing it had turned out to be)
when suddenly he couldn't bear to be there, waiting,
when his friend came home from work
(smiling his thanks at her for making tea,
filling bowls with bombay mix, amusing his weekend guest)
and so, instead, smoothed out their bed, reclaimed his bag,
went out into the driving rain;
took no bearings from the city's re-built zone –
its soul-free phoenix of precincts, ring roads –
and made at least two loops before sitting down
with the shabby faults of a city park,
feeling the ugliness seep in,
absorbing rust, rot and rubbish in the failing light
until the blacked out park decoupled him,
turned him back to where, wondering at the strangeness
of his absence, the anxious friend twitched at curtains
while she carefully sliced an onion for their evening meal,
its thin milk oozing, her nostrils prickling at its scent.

He hesitated on the doorstep as she beckoned him into the lit house,
the tears beading in her eyes misleading him;
followed behind, took a deep breath, prepared his words.

THIRTY PAIRS OF YELLOW EYES

Free, suddenly, to enter every room
we sat, unreproached, in the parlour.
Trying Chesterfield and Chaise Longue,
we stretched and yawned.
Sunlight whirled in pools through the net lace;
jostling for its warmth, we staked our claims early,
inching westwards with the day.
But soon, windows and doors shut fast, the house simmered
and we crept beneath the table, panting.

Blue bottles buzzed.
At first we caught them, nonchalantly, from habit.
Later, we fought for the snap
of silence, the crunch of thorax.
By night we prowled forbidden places,
nudging china from ledges and shelves, scattering your sheet music.
Wanting your touch, we nestled your armpits, kneaded your belly,
pushed our noses hard against your chin.
But you lay still, your scent bitter and strange.

And nobody came.
Curious, unsure, we sniffed; pulled the shawl from your shoulders.
Moving closer, we stalked you out, began to mark you. Spray. Shit.
Nothing happened.
Restless, we circled you slowly,
cautious under each other's gaze.
On the seventh day we approached.
Chose the cold, pale places:
Nose. Ankles. Mouth. Cheeks.

TENNER

We made it from a cornflake packet:
an oblong of card slit from the flap,
then stuck through with drawing pins
(two rows of five) and sealed with sellotape.
Ten little bayonets poised for vertical attack,
their tips skywards.

Testing its scratch on our palms we shuddered and winked.
Passed it on, under the desks, down to the girl in the second row,
sitting behind Wendy Wellcold.
Pull your chair in fat ass, the girl hissed,
and Wendy, quick to please, lifted her thighs (just long enough)
for me to slip the *tenner* under her skirt.

THE VILLAGE

When she was small she had a farm.
Plastic cows grazed, year long, on constant felt,
shiny pigs farrowed every day,
and horses froze fluent in fields.
The farmer, his wife, three children were grouped:
tiny gingham checks against toy fence.
The seasons were kind; this valley yielded
honeycomb, cheese, sweet milk. Everything golden.

Now, older, she has a village.
Look closely.
She moulds a blacksmith from soft clay,
gives him a white hot forge,
then skewers his body on iron bars.
She blesses a baker with sour dough,
fixes the musician (cauliflower ears, finger rags),
arranges the minister in scarlet garters.

This village is hot, excites her:
a novelist remaindered, pulped,
the gambler sunk by a short head,
a drunk sipping camomile tea.
See, she builds a world with her gone god-love:
she puts the teacher in an empty room;
condemns him to blankness.
Silence.

THE BLONDE TRIANGLE

Christmas at Charing Cross station;
office parties streaming out, into the evening.
By the Strand exit I watch three people:
she staggers while they support her,
arms along unfamiliar shoulders.
They are surprised by the feel of blonde hair,
the brush of her body.

I watch the girl's black hat slip down her back.
As she reaches up to rescue it, the one on the left moves
his spare hand down to the centre of her:
the blonde triangle.
He rubs his hand against her, then looks around;
moves it quickly when he sees me,
watching him stealing.

STRUWWELPETER LOVER

You stretched your toes in her corners, rubbed the balls
of your feet where your mother had been.
I lay, rigid with the thought of your father.
Their single beds were swaddlings:
pushed together, bound by tight sheets.
We fastened our mouths on their secrets,
swallowed their heavy scent.

You remembered German bread, her milk,
breath on your cheek as she leant by your head
in white cotton. The shine of her patent shoe,
the tap of her heels on a stripped floor.
These were your sepia stories:
her little boy with haystack curls and pointed finger nails
the Struwwelpeter.

As the birds clawed and flapped above our wild, shock-heads
we plucked feathers from our hair,
scratched dark letters on the backs of our hands.
Then, mummied in narrow sheets, we rolled
towards the struwwelpeter hole between their beds.
Our boots watched from the floor
as you combed my tousled hair with your finger nails.

DER MASS WEIZEN

Today, we take the lime green S2 line
in the direction of Petershause.
I have chosen, without thinking,
a green cotton blouse embroidered with yellow stars.

Our stop is the one after Karlsfeld, just past the Ford factory
and the big houses with swimming pools.
I hadn't expected people to be living here,
am surprised by their laughing gardens, as the train rolls by.

You have been dry, now, for ten weeks.
We are on holiday, making our slow way
past mountains, cathedrals, sliding rivers.
You have unpacked your pills, nightly, at each hotel.

You sweat and tremble, pointing to places
you remember. This is your country;
but unfamiliar to walk, too quickly in the heat,
past the kiosks and cafes.

For the last bit of this journey we take a bus.
It is full of American voices, Japanese cameras,
a few people wearing headscarves.
It was my idea to come here.

We climb off and stand aside, let the others tramp in lines
along a narrow track, the gravel underfoot unbearable against the silence.
There is no shelter here from the high sun;
it burns through the thin fabric on my shoulders.

The crowd troop to the sheds (to see for themselves)
while we walk the perimeter, looking for a gate.
I stare upwards at the barbs along four lines of wire above our heads,
a white concrete tower with four small windows in its roof.

I stumble, slip as the gravel skitters away
under my smooth-worn soles. Out of water,
our lips begin to crack. Beside me you are walking,
as always, with a stoop, trying not to be so tall,

as if you have no right to be here.
You lift your anxious eyes to mine
and I turn away, thinking how ragged
you look today, with your sunken cheeks.

And I wonder, then, if this is your country,
if, perhaps, you live with these walls
and watch towers, and the gravel,
crunching and sliding underfoot.

Later (arriving back in Munich too late
to leave by the early evening train)
you head for a Biergarten;
order ein Viertel Liter und Mass Weizen.

RUSSELL, KANSAS

We find our friend living in a dot and italics
on page 39 of your map.
I run my fingers across the Sacramento Valley,
scanning ahead to turnings in a road
I once travelled with someone else.

How the sky straddled us as we crawled
through these small towns:
this road shimmered in the pooling heat,
the wheat parting before us,
as we crossed our twenty second State.

We made page 40 by dusk.
As I re-trace the half-forgotten route
my fingers stumble on a name so faint,
(not even dotted on your map)
that transports me, beyond mere memory,

to a nowhere land where, outside town,
we stopped the car, lay flat in the grass,
then rolled, like children, down a bank.
And I turned and I turned, in the blue stripes
of his shirt, I turned, as the sky wheeled on me,

converged in continuous blue on me,
in *Russell*, Kansas.
And as, from nowhere, you say *I love you*
I hear across the years and miles that other man,
shouting it into the skies.

And then the spinning stops:
a cloud outside slices through my silence,
mocking my long-gone heaven-cries,
and the grass stills under a flat sky.
I close the book, get up from your bed.

NOT THERE

The therapist says:
Clench your fists, then let them go. Close your eyes. Picture happiness.

I spool a desert; rocky outcrops thread red needles
across the sun and my elbow burns through glass
as we drive to the creek.
(I am not there: not *precisely* there)

I frame a mountain; Bristlecone Pines fringe a glass lake
at tree line and I gasp, twisting in thin air
as we hike into sky.
(I am not there: not *exactly* there)

I freeze a river; you carry me through, to an island,
jeans hitched to your knees,
then lift me gently from your back.
I hear you say: *Good. That's lovely* and I open my eyes.

But you are still not there.

THE VENTRILOQUIST

While the sticky fingers and taunting mouths arrive,
I look out from behind red velvet.
On this stage I will be silenced: struck dumb,
with only my hand to signal to the crowds.

As the children snake towards me,
eager for the little man who will sit on my knee,
I recall my father: the way he
would take me on his lap, hands hidden from view,

fingering secrets for me to keep.
A child looks up, shouts. I retreat.
I want to haul that little boy across the years
and make him speak.

But I must go on: throw my voice away.
The little men keep my silence in a box.

FEVER

Two days, I lay, on twisted sheets:
belly, thighs, breasts glistening.

I haunt north London streets again;
here is glass in my foot, the blood black on my shoe,
and you, stooping to kiss my back
as you fix the hook on my dress;
here is a railway station, tracks sliding away,
your face buried in my hair.
These are the fires of strangers:
a glance, a hand, words snagging on small agonies.

On the third day, through miles of wire,
you thread me these: camomile, honey, kiss.

GRUNDLAGE

You call on a Saturday, while the kids are out, your voice a whisper.
I balance the phone against my ear to light a cigarette.
I can't go on, can't make it right, I hear you say,
the grundlage is all wrong.

Grundlage? I ask.
You search for words, stumbling on your mother tongue,
decide, finally, on 'foundation'.
Then leave, I say.

But the line goes dead and my words coil to ground.
I listen to the rattle of a Bakerloo line train
and think of her. Then try to picture you,
the children (playing outside).

YOUR SILENCE

That night, I took off my clothes;
stood before you, offering my upturned breasts and mouth,
then walked into your arms.

This woman was trembling: a single rose
in your arms, lifting your head to a flickering light
and the shower of tears.

Tonight, I watch my breath;
I want to see how you arranged her.
Is it crystal? Your buttonhole? The sour milk bottle?

Or perhaps she is lying with the debris of leavings,
abandoned with the cigarette ends
and empty glasses?

Should I pour water through the telephone lines?
Send sachets of cut flower food in the mail?
Or will my silence stop her dying?

RESPONDENT

The week the baby was born his wife petitioned for divorce.
The new mother should not think herself the first, or that she would last,
and there were particulars she wanted her to know.

The Respondent had behaved unreasonably.
He had *promised her that he would improve,*
be faithful to her,
but had *relationships with a number of women*
which *caused the Petitioner extreme distress.*
He had *disappeared for days at a time,*
taken a lover *for two or three years,*
moved in with a mistress.

It was their second Christmas but their first tree.
Cheeks flushed, stamping the balls of their feet,
they clatter through the door with lights and baubles.
In the corner, the answer phone is glowing red.
She starts to warm some milk, presses *play.*

On several occasions other women telephoned
asking for the Respondent...

She cross-threads the top of the baby's bottle several times,
trying to explain the voice unspooling
around her kitchen, her baby, her Christmas lights,
speaking his familiar name, carefully holding back the words,
swallowing sobs.

Eventually the Respondent was forced to accept
that the Petitioner knew about this relationship...

All she can find is his back, shoulders pulled up high around his lowered,
listening head as he fiddles with the cooker hood.

The Respondent made the Petitioner feel paranoid
for suspecting that he was having a relationship...

Later, when she forced some words from the back of her throat,
he said they were entirely unreasonable.

THE HOLE

Today I turned over the worms.
Beneath a thin tree I bit ground
(dug into the silence, fixed my eyes on tight buds,
exposed white roots and, angrily, dug deeper).

A sharp January morning.
Panting slightly, my breath lacing the air,
I leaned my chest, harder, against the smooth wooden bar.
The blade suddenly scraped concrete.

I had found the bottom of our world, where the garden began,
and where this digging, this frantic hole, had to end.

GENNARO GAGLIANO

He was toying with giving it up,
lured by the challenge of *directing* events.
He'd bowed and fingered every possible string of notes,
had led and followed, played alone, in major and minor
auditoria across the world.
So he understood enough to be patient with the highly-charged;
could coax nightingales from pearly throats,
warm the public with wit and charm.
And he liked not having to carry it around;
had become tired of it always being there –
to take care of, to worry about.

But, unsure, he still worked the circuit:
Europe, South America, the Far East –
Durham, birthland of sea and mines.
A familiar place for him to play
but dissonant at 1.20 a.m. as, weary with late food,
he heads for the mouth of the railway viaduct,
the north east wind making bad percussion of his step.
Under the arches, now, he strains to make out
the strange shape ahead:
slows, then, at the horror of his car boot
(the boot where he had tiredly left it)
gaping empty in the night.

He'd been toying with giving it up for weeks
but didn't sleep, now, for two months:
drove around mining villages posting messages for its return
(the police advised caution: £1000);
hired an undercover agent (local chap);
was featured on Crimewatch (BBC); went global on The Internet.
When all his leads went cold and silent
he turned the car radio up loud; drove back to London
to pick up the threads of festival administration.
But at night lay awake,
twisting strands of horse hair through guilty hands,
dreaming its touch, its shape –
knowing he couldn't play on anything else.

Living quietly in Ham with cats and parrots,
a medium, when told that he had lost something (nothing more)
said it would certainly come back to him,
that 3 and 5 were good numbers,
and described a railway viaduct
(although she'd never visited Durham).
He slept a little that night;
dreaming digits, translating numbers into notes.
And in the morning – the 5th of that month – the phone call came.
Found On Sale in a record shop in Sunderland (£150).

He drove non-stop to be re-united:
amazed at the news that 3 men had taken it,
amused by the fact that nobody had bought it,
but mostly quiet – driving in silence this time – to reclaim his violin.
Arriving at 1.20 p.m., a stone's throw from where he'd been born,
he carefully wiped the sweat from his hands, took possession.
Tomorrow, he will change the wording for his publicity;
draw attention to the fact that he plays
on a very fine Gennaro Gagliano violin of 1768.

SUN, LONDON W10

I have watched it rot in Mexico and slide into the ocean;
tried to haul it back on puppet strings.

I have walked with its ripeness in Indiana:
a red ball and half dollar in my hands.

I have wept beneath it on Windmill Hill:
a gold ring spinning our forever goodbye.

I have waited for it to rise on Sinai:
faint disc trembling in an egg-shell sky.

I have wanted it here,
where dust motes fall through shafts of light.

THE CONCRETE

It's late, almost midnight, and we are driving in rain.
You are talking at me:
the concrete, you say, *not the abstract,*
the particular, not the general.

Do you remember how this night the M4 was closed at Southall?
And how I drove us home the strangest way
past Ealing, Acton, Park Royal, Willesden
and then through Harlesden, north west London?

November '91. The lights had gone out
and they were burning cardboard boxes in the street,
flames spiralling upwards. Can you recall the car,
crawling slowly towards the figures in the road?

The way flames lit the face of an old man, crouching?
My heart thumped as the lights turned red and we had to wait
by that junction for them to change, with the glass shattering
and faces staring in through our windows.

After, driving to your Notting Hill end of Ladbroke Grove
(sweeping, tree lined) I thought about how the abstracts –
anomie, alienation – translate to faces and flames,
while you talked about nothing in particular.

II WALKING ON TIPTOE

He needs to stand on tiptoes that hopes to touch the moon.

Thomas Fuller, The Holy State and The Profane State (1642)

THIS VERDANT GRASS

The tired words lose currency;
recast as cliché, well-worn images flatten to platitude.
And yet no other word was quite precise, exact that day
when suddenly, rising at the left of us, startling from the razed land,
ochre – a mountain of it;
the dug mustardy millstone grit of Derbyshire
heaped to a mighty scar, yards from our track.

We circled it, closing in,
the sandy dust settling on our boots,
to discover two scooped holes tunnelling into ancient earth,
a flurry of prints around their mouths.
We turned away, saying how conspicuous, how terribly vulnerable.
Intruders, we made to leave,
stumbled back towards the path.

Then at the perimeter, where the ochre ran out,
it caught my eye: grass so unnaturally bright,
so vivid, so beyond green.
Dazzled, I looked ahead to the moorland track,
compared its pale reseda with this brilliant emeraldine;
searched vainly, then, for a better word to describe this grass.

You showed me fresh dung: the nitrogen explained it.
Find a badger, then, to give you back meaning,
to weigh a word with a heap of earth;
then dig the univocal from a cliché, hone the fresh, plain coinage –
this stuff about not putting *verdant* grass in a poem is shit.

WILD GEESE*

Trawl my baby's soul through squally skies,
Unseen wish hounds calling through the dawn.
Flesh stand cold when hell-bound geese baptise.

Harrow mist, with sighing wings, wring cries
From marsh and tarn, mother and new born.
Trawl my baby's soul through squally skies.

Light break on the arctic fowl she flies,
Bearing her north into autumn morn.
Flesh stand cold when hell-bound geese baptise.

Quiver the fens as you harmonise
The dirge you squawk for the one I mourn.
Trawl my baby's soul through squally skies.

Limpidly, mutely, from chastened eyes,
Old griefs and barnacled tears are drawn.
Flesh stand cold when hell-bound geese baptise.

Child be bathed in waters at sunrise,
Your name called, from ululations torn.
Trawl my baby's soul through squally skies.
Flesh stand cold when hell-bound geese baptise.

* In British legend, the northward migration of wild geese is connected with the
conducting to the icy Northern Hell of the souls of unbaptised infants. The sound
of the geese passing unseen overhead is supposed to be made by the wish hounds.

LUMP

I hadn't bothered to check them;
never seemed any point.
So many different ways of touching,
so many hands.
I remember mouths too:
different tongues and teeth.
They weren't looking for this;
wouldn't have known it.

You tell me it is large.
3.5 centimetres you say.
Mobile. Hard.
You make me lift my arm,
dig your clever fingers in the dark stubble.
Then you sit me up,
lift my right breast gently.
It is in the centre, you say.

I walk to my office and search for letters to sign.
I want to send them off, finish things.
In the drawer I find a ruler
and thumb at black notches;
they are cruel and exact against my milky skin.
These are lines to live with.

SMOOTHNESS

A half cantaloupe:
flesh firm across my bones,
smooth as fingers against the shell of an egg
or ice in silk.

A breast once heavy with wasted milk:
the body of a baby, her lips still,
and the years stretching away,
puckering the brown disc with fine hairs, a perfect mole.

Did mother-love turn my nipple inside out?
The craggy pap sent plumb-lines down,
knotting a crevice in the pink
to sound a lump.

Now, it turns on smoothness:
a needle glittering in the back of my hand,
the man in green, his knife sliding to cut,
the flesh splitting.

AUTUMN IN GEORGIA

The June egg divided in Tel-Aviv as I swam,
alone in the sea, watching a mother
dance with her child in the sand.
In Jerusalem, street nerves pulsed,
stung by frantic shots from a single gun:
the faces were taut, expectant.
When is an arab a Palestinian? Or an egg a child?

In London, sick with waiting for red to seep,
I squeezed the urine, drop by drop,
and watched the vial turn pink.
On Channel 4 great rivers flood,
their long names tumbling from our lips:
M-i-double s-i-double s-i-double p-i.
How does childhood end? With a breaking of river banks?

I go south and wait with the gulls,
pace the shore where they breed
in the ribs of a disconnected pier.
The radio signals, locates the displaced:
it crackles of Serbia, Croatia,
the concepts are nation and state.
Where do we fix our boundaries? Whom can we host?

You dial my number, pouring tears,
paring my moon belly with your thin words,
your cry, *I reject this child... not wanted.*
Here, on shingle, a far country trembles in my ear:
A rouble is no longer worth a rouble, in Georgia,
where they are setting their boundaries against exile.
I stand on the edge of this land, with my child.

MALE

He thrust deeper,
battered the cervix to make her bleed,
gave her heavy things to carry,
said she would be sacked.

After the birth,
she fingers the whorl of blond hair at its crown,
feels thin lips fasten at her breast,
stares into the ghost of his eyes.

When she changes the child,
and the ruched white skin unfolds in innocence,
she remembers the hard bulb of his father, glistening.
Lays her head in his wetness.

GONE
for Dylan Ariel

I am waiting for you to speak
as you sprawl, staring at the wooden gull above my bed.
I tilt my head in your face, try my smile
and imagine you mouthing *wing, bird, fly.*

You draw your knees into a silent curl
then haul yourself to stand against the trembling wall,
throb your tongue against your lips and stumble on the rush of air.
I want you to speak my name, or claim your own, clear and full.

I remember finding my first word:
smoky cellophane crackled in my fingers as I unwrapped
the pages of a pink quilt book to discover father's insect letters –
my *first smile, first steps* creeping along their dotted lines.

And there I knew my whole life through a single word: *Gone.*
Could my world, my all gone world, have started there?
What did I know, in such few months, to name this loss?
I pull you to me, hold you tight, chant these words in your ear:

Here, Now, Yes.

ATTIC WINDOW

Attic window where she hung a white gull,
wanting its call across the sky, waves on a pebble beach.

In her landlocked house
she makes it fly for the baby, crying:
eeyeek eeyeek eeyeek.
She doesn't think about his father
but she misses the dark blue line at the edge of the world,
distant ships, shingle, high clouds.

Attic window pounded by rain,
knowing she loved him as it slid away in sheets.

She told him, when he asked, that what she really wanted
was to see the sea again. He said that he would take her
if she would walk with him into the hills.
She turned all night beneath her sloping square of sky,
waiting for light to break the breathless night,
fearing the beat of water drumming on glass, her heart's tattoo.

Attic window framing the stars as they lay,
searching for silver, counting to seven.

Alone, she didn't notice things beyond the window,
thought only about what she could no longer see.
But he points through the pane at the Plough,
tells her why it drifts across the glass
into a perfect frame by three a.m.
She sees a kite in the sky. Catches the string, lets it go.

Attic window where they leaned out into black air
the night the comet came.

After their baby is born
they open the window wide, fold their waists across the sill.
Scanning the sky for trailing lights,
they hoist their daughter up;
name her Ursa for the seven stars,
Isis for their splintering moon.

Attic window where the earth passed between
the moon and the sun.

Tonight she cries for her baby, remembering white lights
sparkling at the edge of the sea
the night he was born.
Just after midnight, a shadow creeps across the moon
and she thinks the light will go out entirely.
But he holds her tight, points to light inside the dark circle,
a perfect disc burning orange in the sky.

WALKING ON TIPTOE

That afternoon, a pale amber light lit the tops of the hills
as we drove home from work and I felt myself unfurl to greet it,
grow brave after months of darkness.
I started to talk about him, that evening, while you chose a video
and the new baby kicked on the rug.
There was just something that didn't feel right.
I could live longer without words, if it was only that,
but there were the cars which he clutched
and the things which he moved, backwards and forwards,
the route home from work which couldn't be changed.
I asked you to get down the medical dictionary
and said: *Look up Autism, read me that.*

In a strong, steady voice you read to me from the living room
while I moved quietly around the kitchen, making his tea.
I listened, vaguely, to the symptoms and signs,
thinking 'yes' and 'yes' again but not really engaging,
knowing the same could be said of all two year olds:
don't want to look, don't want to be picked up, don't want to play or talk.
So I wasn't desperately listening to you – was busy with a saucepan –
when you read, without hesitation (as if the words had no meaning):
There may be other behavioural abnormalities, such as walking on tiptoe…

No, No, No. The pan clattered against the sink. You continued reading.
Backwards and forwards, I paced the kitchen, flapping my arms.
No need for more words. *Stop, Stop* I yelled at you and you ran to me,
then, spinning on the spot, not knowing where to turn,
how to get back, back to where I was before.
I banged my wrists hard against the glass in the patio doors,
wailing *No, No, No* as the light went out of the sky.
Inside, the genie was out of the lamp.
But oh to be free I heard him say as my son sat,
trapped in the glow from the screen, fixed by the colours.
I turned myself to the hills, switched on the outside light,
stared at the garden.

Later, when you understood, you smashed your fist against the wall.
The switch cracked from the bottom corner to the top right.
The next day you unscrewed the fissured plate, fitted new parts, fixed it up.

CHERRY LIPS

When we came home from the hospital
everything was different.
Each night you would get up with me,
bring tea, and sit on the edge of the bed, watching.
But we suffered by day for those fractured nights
and soon I said that you shouldn't bother to get up every time –
that you couldn't really help.
And so you brought me things to read.

In the pile by the bed I find *John Body's Fine Woodworking Catalogue,*
its pages roughly turned, stained with
circles of coffee and your scribings.
You are looking for a saw to make a picture frame
and fix our fleeting glimpse of her in glass and wood.
I consider the precision of a mitre joint
as her sapwood newness cleaves to me
and the Plough scatters light.

I leaf the pages for a wood, offering lumber to the night.
My breath ghosts the glass as I season timber
then shave the creams of Apple and Beech,
chisel the hard grain of Laurel and Pear.
I carve through the straightness of Lime,
hewing hours from the Sycamore's ripple.
I turn the wind through Macassar Ebony,
hurl Walnut burrs across the sky.

Under the moon's gaze I wax Cedar,
polish Yew while the stars shake,
and, by the time I pluck my nipple
from her Cherry lips,
I have whittled it to a sliver of Ash.
The Holly's whiteness
laps my bright circle
as sun and moon dovetail.

TOE-WALKING

You could be forgiven for thinking
that I avoid the chill of kitchen tiles,
lift my arches from ungiving stone.
I have seen the crawling baby do this:
straighten her legs, lift up on her toes,
not to feel the hardness against her knees or soles.

But, if you pay attention, you will see me
walk like this through yielding grass,
mince across an Indian rug.
I do not raise myself because the world
is cold or hard but for its sake:
to feel blood under pressure,
whiteness spreading across the balls of my feet,
to have my heels off the ground,
not to be taller or to help me see, but only for this:
the smallest connection I can make with the world.

There is a knack of course: lean too far forward
and the toe tips squeeze, pulling against tendons.
My balance is perfect, my parents say.
It is months of practice: walking on tiptoe, high kicking.
It isn't obligate is it? the neurologist said,
as I varied my step in his office one day.
No: this is my fix. Mine, mine, mine.

EAR INFECTION

I am not saying that this caused it.
It may have been the secret genes
of his tight-lipped 'natural' father
(another skeleton son in an expensive cupboard-school);
or the vaccine-loaded needle the GP pushed into his legs;
it may have been the 72 hours I laboured,
offering him the o-ring world slow centimetre by centimetre.
I cannot be absolutely sure of cause.
But, when I knew, had a name for all that was not right,
it was those three days, three nights merging that I thought about.

Here alone, brimming with a second child,
I was filling sticky syringes with banana medicine,
counting the headscan out (103, 104...),
fanning his hot red face, laying on lukewarm cloths.
This small child with the legs he had only just found,
swaying like a drunk, stumbling across hard tiles
to where I stood, holding desperately on to my life
(solid, dependable objects: tea bag, tap, kettle). Turned at his cry,
scooped that small body back to live those days by me:
no fluid, no food, no sleep. Until, on the third day, it was over.

Neither of us thought much about it after,
when he didn't speak.
Didn't puzzle when he stopped showing us the pictures in his books,
preferring to sort things out and line them up –
yellows, blues, reds.
Didn't connect that by the time his sister was born
he could barely point or wave.
But, later, swallowing the bitter pill of diagnosis,
I took the sickly forever lozenge
remembering those three jumbled days and nights.

I am not saying this caused it
but that tonight I am gripped frozen, benumbed:
unable to hold my 15 month daughter,
her burning body familiar,
the high whine crazing my scalp as she refuses,
the way her brother did, dose after dose.
It is the same pain I weep with, the same exhaustion
of the same three nights without sleep –
their lives same, fusing, and the difference me:
the fear re-wiring my mother love, unwomanning my hands, arms, head.

GREEN VELVET DRESS

The cheque from the local arts board is for childcare.
I footle around, collecting abandoned toys,
discovering dust, a cracked tile, loose buttons –
things you can't take care of when you're busy
chanting poems to your children.
A strange muse, this absence. Maybe mine
would answer better to a day at Salisbury races, high up in the Tattersalls,
losing every pound by a short head while swallows drift across the eaves.
Or taking the next flight to Boston, just to drift slowly down
over Logan's curling harbour.
I could arrange for crates of champagne to be delivered every week,
sit in the garden bubbling poems,
or give the cash away, in 50s, to the night shift –
interrupt, just briefly, the clang of dropping steel across the valley.
I should buy a velvet dress, green as a forest, to ripple as I walk,
with a nap so close you would run your hands, gently, down every fibre.

THE LITTORAL ZONE

This is the littoral zone, you say, as we scavenge below strandline,
picking out shells and weeds for the children.
You lift a dogwhelk, turn it in long-fingered hands,
place it gently on your palm. *Hermit Crab,* you whisper,
as the barnacled shell rolls over, sprouts a pincer.
Gull-eyed, you pluck a tiny periwinkle from the sandy flats,
show me a speck of crab curled inside,
explaining it will leave this for a bigger shell in time.
This recluse, this little anchorite, is in the first shell of its life:
strung out ahead of it, across this Breton beach, a future of univalves.

I like that, I tell you:
the thought of wearing a right-sized shell
with room enough to grow; getting the fit right –
feeling snug (but not too much).
And I realise, as I say this, that I've been crawling backwards,
reversing across the littoral zone –
cramping into ever smaller shells.

We heat the periwinkle with my lighter
until the *Decapod Crustacean* looses grip.
It would, you say, resist and break in two if pulled;
I think of larger shells which I have lost.
Exposed, its soft abdomen, naked tail spirals in your palm.
I watch it search. Unguarded, in peril, any shelter will do;
I have drawn myself up, folded myself over and over,
flattened into too-tight shells to escape such fire.
This ascetic needs room. You offer it back the shell, beach it.
It will slowly grow there, now, you say.

I starfish down beside it, face to the sun, stretch fingers and toes
in sand while you run our children to the waves.
I roll over, feel the soft under-belly of warm sand,
the breeze of a carapace sky. I fill my lungs, cry with the gulls.
Here, with you, I can uncurl and not touch shell:
the stifled, muffled noise of mouth pushed on periwinkle
becomes a voice again.

ECCLESALL WOODS

I need to enter them at a particular place
so drive twice along the road until I am sure.
We unload children, plunge into the Sunday wood,
Dylan dancing ahead, squinting up at the leaking canopy.
I want to walk the way my grandmother took me through these woods;
trace her route across the stream, up a bank,
stride out, briskly, leaves crunching. *Don't drag your feet,*
she'd reprimand, *let's keep in step.*
I try to remember, take cues from twisting roots,
but her great-grandson side-tracks again,
tilts his face to the singing trees, lures me away.

In a home for old people, face to the hills, she is dying,
moving slowly from Zimmerframe, to chair, to bed.
Several times we are called; set our anxious faces
against the frail shoulders which rise from thin sheets,
the fine lines that claw across her drying skin.
We sit for a while. Hold the children close to her face.
Driving away, I am asking whether she will live long enough
to hear at least one of our children talk, when you swerve suddenly,
try to dodge the bird flying low across our path.
It slams black against the windscreen, catapults onto the road,
and you pull over, run back. I wait with the children,
watch through the wing mirror as you cup it to the reservoir edge.
A fledgling. Broken neck.

When the last call comes, I drive to find her curtains closed,
the room lit by a damask rose glow from the lamp she never used.
I pull back the sheets to hold her hand;
someone has opened them, folded her arms into a kiss across her chest.
I run my fingers slowly along her shoulders, tracing the bones.
I have never been this close to her, this familiar.
Later, in the chapel, it is the straightness of her neck I notice,
rising perfectly from swathes of white and purple lace.
I follow a coffin (which seems too small) down from the hills,
thinking about the blackbird, the trees singing in Ecclesall Woods,
and my past imperfect memory of those interwoven roots,
the path I can't remember to the hollow.

PRINTS

After she died, we got a tripod.
It's easy, now, to take a family shot; to edge the camera into place
and race back, grabbing a child each as the red pulse
quickens to a flash at the laughing family falling into view.

Without the tripod, it hadn't been so easy to compose
this simple gift for Christmas (the one that turned out to be her last)
so the plain frame we had chosen stayed empty until Christmas Eve
when, out of time, we shuffled through the latest batch;

settled on one we both agreed was *not so bad*
(although the red-eyed devil baby ridiculed our sweet smiles,
her brother's blankness seemed stamped across his silent brow).
We would, we said, put it in *for now*.

But, once given, the print proved impossible to remove.
It passed the whole of winter wrapped in a hanky on her lap,
her slim fingers uncovering our faces,
tracing our hair, shoulders, printing the glass,

then rubbing hard with white cotton, catching her own spun-whorls
of handkerchief lace against the picture's wooden frame.
And, as she weakened, took to her bed, its sharp right angles
jutted out from beneath her lavender sheets.

At the end, the warden eased it from her; stood it beside the bed.
So it came back to me with other gifts: the scarf for her shoulders,
scented drawer liners, olive wood from Jerusalem.
I found the photo beautiful now: smudged, transformed by her prints.

At home, I propped it on a high shelf, glanced now and then
as I walked by. Until today, startled by sunlight, I stood gazing
at glass glinting where the new cleaner (just doing her job)
must have rubbed and rubbed at Grandma's fingerprints.

THE CLOTH

I find this small detail in the warp and weft of your life,
an observation buried amid the fact and fabrication,
the stories and speculation we sift and search for something
to explain the way they glittered, those words you rode:
their horizons ringing us still, red-eyed, echoing.

Did you take it clean from a drawer
where it might have covered the first rising of your next loaf?
Or was it a muslin square of sour milk carried, that last day,
beneath the baby on your shoulder? Or did you choose this one
because it was too filmy, too threadbare, to be trusted in the door?

Did you fold it precisely, the creases firmly edged
by the fingers which had finally put down their pen,
leaked last griefs like shredded red balloons?
And what did it protect from the hardness of your oven floor?
Did you tuck it underneath your chin? Against your jaw?

Or was it the tender place, your temple,
where those blue lights had burned ten years before,
sliding the glass shut, sealing your air?
Was it the scar-side you chose to lay at rest,
in this deliberate act of reverence and respect:

the placing of your head upon a cloth?
And did its softness give you back your shore:
a vision of sea dripping, wrung clear as a bell
from that tiny pillow, moon and stars trembling,
the world shaking from your oar?

FATHER

While I cut a sheet of paper into strips
and write out messages – one from each of us –
their father stretches the gaudy nylon across a slender frame.

For less than a fiver it comes with tails and twine;
I follow the diagram to attach them, remembering the way string
was always too short, or missing, when I was a child.

We tumbled through drawers and cupboards, then,
hunting for bits to knot together and wind
onto the fishing reel used to fly our home-grown kites.

These were my father's prototypes: pencil sketches transformed
into lengths of splintered wood, bound into fantastic frames
with sticky tape, then decked with fabric from my mother's box.
The question was not *How High?* but *Would it fly?*

Today, the children watch while I work the kite into the brooding sky,
running from side to side, letting it out over gorse and scrub.
It's light, catches the breezes, tugs easily from me.

High enough, now, I explain how to fasten a message to the string,
pull the twine taut with my spare hand, then let the slip of paper go.
I urge it upwards, shouting to the children as it docks with the kite.

As we cast the others off, I remember how magical it seemed to me
when my father's kites flew messages through the clouds.
I count the years, make him 64. I missed his birthday this month.

Living closer than before, we have gathered distance like let-go kites;
I track the pink and yellow diamond as it trawls the steely sky;
sinuous tendril unfurling whoops of grandchild joy (that will not carry),
mending messages (the tethered, grounded words we don't let fly).

INTO THE BLUE

I

He is a diviner:
his body shakes at the prospect
as he veers swiftly from my side, flapping and trembling,

to silent springs bubbling from underground.
He has led me to still fountains, hidden wells and troughs;
searches through his picture books for all his lakes and lochs.

I have often felt an urge, in seas and pools, to loose my grip, let him go;
have wanted to unclip his spinning arms
and watch a perfect butterfly emerge.

Have fancied he would skim easily
across the water,
pollen balanced on dancing wings.

II

Tonight, after dark, I drive alone;
hesitate at the brow of the hill
(lose clutch point, roll back, try again).

Inside, I undress slowly.
I am not sure what I am doing there;
unfamiliar, now, quite changed.

But I lower myself in, strike out;
discover sheets, then, sliding across the blades of my shoulders
as palms slice in remembered angles and limbs rise through

the breasted swell.
And tears roll down my cheeks as I feel my legs,
become aware of an ache in my back,

and of this silence –
language caught in a funnel of green space,
the voices hanging above me.

And I strike out, again, for the deep
with the straight white lines wobbling below me
and the crescent moon tippling its light

over my sleeping butterfly child
could swim, forever, tonight,
into the blue.

ELIZABETH BARRETT

Elizabeth Barrett and Dylan

Photograph: Vic Lally

Born in Sheffield in 1961, Elizabeth Barrett studied for her BA and PhD (in Modern History and Politics) at the University of London. While an undergraduate she won a scholarship to the University of Massachusetts at Amherst, taking courses there and at Smith College, Northampton. She later trained as an English teacher, subsequently working in educational research and as a University Lecturer in Education.

Elizabeth Barrett is recognised as a rising poetic talent. Her writing has been published in a wide range of magazines and anthologies and she has been placed in a number of poetry competions. She was a featured writer in *New Voices 2* (Dale Press, 1995) which collects 18 of her poems. *Walking on Tiptoe*, the winning poetry collection for the 1998 Staple First Editions Award, is a powerful and sensitive representation of personal and interpersonal life in (and out of) a family, one of whose members is autistic. In 1997 the title poem of this collection was nominated for the Forward Prize in the category 'best individual poem'.

In 1994 Elizabeth Barrett returned to Sheffield, where she lives with her husband and two young children. She has recently given up her academic career in order to devote more time to her children and writing.

ACKNOWLEDGEMENTS

Some of the poems in this collection, or earlier versions of them, first appeared in *Stand Magazine, The Wide Skirt, The New Writer, The Honest Ulsterman, London Magazine, The Rialto, Envoi,* Staple, *Fatchance, Scratch, Rustic Rub, Poetry Nottingham, Smiths Knoll* and *First Time.* Other poems in this collection appeared in the anthologies *Stretching It A Touch* (1997); *New Voices* (1994); *Ice on the Wing* (1993); *Dance on the Horizon* (1993) and *New Worlds* (1992).

Wild Geese won first prize in the Hastings Open Poetry Competition (1992); *Your Silence* won second prize in the Berkshire Open Poetry Competition (1992); *Mrs Egon Schiele's Complaint* won fourth prize in the Cardiff International Poetry Competition (1993); *Green Velvet Dress* was commended in the Dulwich Festival Poetry Competition (1997).

Some of the poems were written with the assistance of a *New Beginnings Writers Award* from Yorkshire and Humberside Arts.

Thanks are due to Malcolm Layfield, whose story inspired *Gennaro Gagliano.*

Staple New Writing

A non-profit-making company, limited by guarantee.

Staple magazine, established 1982, is published in March, July and December of each year. Subscription details and Guidelines are available from the address below. Individual submissions – poems and stories – are welcome, but we regret that unsolicited collections cannot be considered.

Tor Cottage, 81 Cavendish Road, Matlock, Derbyshire DE4 3HD

David Lightfoot	LAST ROUND	1991
Jennifer Olds	THE HALF-ACRE RANCH	1992
Peter Cash	FEN POEMS	1992
Adrienne Brady Ted Burford John Latham Paul Munden David Winwood	QUINTET	1993
Donna Hilbert	WOMEN WHO MAKE MONEY AND THE MEN WHO LOVE THEM	1994
Jennifer Olds	AN EXTRA HALF-ACRE	1995
Julia Casterton Tobias Hill Joan Jobe Smith Huw Watkins Howard Wright Alicia Yerburgh	SESTET	1995
Gregory Warren Wilson	PRESERVING LEMONS	1996
Ruth Sharman Alison Spritzler-Rose Catherine Conzato John Gower	TWO + TWO	1997
Elizabeth Barrett	WALKING ON TIPTOE	1998